A GUIDE TO JEWISH PRACTICE

WELCOMING CHILDREN

A GUIDE *to* JEWISH PRACTICE

Center for Jewish Ethics
Reconstructionist Rabbinical College
in cooperation with the
Reconstructionist Rabbinical Association

Reconstructionist Rabbinical College Press

1299 Church Road, Wyncote, PA 19095-1898
www.rrc.edu

WELCOMING CHILDREN

RICHARD HIRSH

Dedication

A Guide to Jewish Practice: Welcoming Children is dedicated to my children, Shira Tova and Nadav Yaron, who remind me daily that welcoming children is a life-long blessing.

Richard Hirsh

The blessing "When Holding a Newborn Child for the First Time" (page 69) has been reprinted with permission from *Kol Haneshamah Shirim Uverachot*. The other blessings on pages 67–70 have been reprinted with permission from the *Reconstructionist Rabbinical Association Rabbis Manual*.

Reconstructionist Rabbinical College Press
Wyncote, Pennsylvania

Composition by G&H Soho, Inc.

ISBN 978-0-938945-13-0

2005935343

Printed in the U.S.A.

Contents

Commentators and Advisory Committee *vii*

Preface *ix*

INTRODUCTION 3

PROLOGUE:
"IDENTITY," "STATUS"
AND "DESCENT" 6

WELCOMING CHILDREN 10

THE CONCEPT OF COVENANT 14

P'RU UR'VU: PROCREATION
AS A PRIMARY VALUE 16

CONCEPTION, PREGNANCY,
CHILDBIRTH AND WEANING 21

CIRCUMCISION 25

Brit Mila: *The Covenant of Circumcision* *25*

Hospital Circumcision *32*

Questioning Circumcision *35*

COVENANTAL CEREMONIES
FOR GIRLS 39

Issues of Gender, Exclusion and Inclusion *39*

Rituals of Welcoming and Naming *42*

NAMING 44
Naming and Identity 44
Choosing a Name 46
Names of the Parent/s 49
Naming When One Parent is Not Jewish 50

ADOPTION 52
Adoption in Jewish Tradition 52
Adoption and Conversion 54
Differences of Opinion 55
Adoption and Naming 59
Pidyon Haben: *Redemption of the Firstborn Son* 60

CONCLUSION 63

For Further Reading 65

Prayers and Blessings 67

Biographies of the Contributors 71

Index 73

Commentators

Benjamin Barnett (B.B.)
Kevin Bernstein (K.B.)
Daniel Goldman Cedarbaum (D.G.C.)
Richard Hirsh (R.H.)
Myriam Klotz (M.K.)
Ilyse S. Kramer (I.K.)
Nina H. Mandel (N.H.M.)
Barbara Rosman Penzner (B.R.P.)
Simcha Raphael (S.R.)
Yael Ridberg (Y.R.)
Sandy Eisenberg Sasso (S.E.S.)
Jacob J. Staub (J.J.S.)
David A. Teutsch (D.A.T.)
Abigail B. Weinberg (A.B.W.)

Advisory Committee

Rabbis Richard Hirsh and David Teutsch, *Co-chairs*
Rabbi Lester Bronstein
Deborah Dash Moore, Ph.D.
Chayim Herzig-Marx
Leah Kamionkowski
Tamar Kamionkowski, Ph.D.
Rabbi Nina Mandel
Rabbi Yael Ridberg
Rabbi Jacob Staub

Preface

A Guide to Jewish Practice: Welcoming Children is part of a series of booklets (including *A Guide to Jewish Practice: The Journey of Mourning* [2006]) that will eventually be incorporated into a full volume entitled *A Guide to Jewish Practice: The Life-Cycle.* That volume in turn will be one part of a projected three-part collection, with one volume devoted to values, ethics and daily practice, one volume focusing on the stages of life, and one volume on Shabbat and the Jewish holidays. *A Guide to Jewish Practice* represents Reconstructionist approaches to the opportunities, challenges and issues of living a creative, progressive and spiritually meaningful Jewish life in the 21st century.

The *Guide* project was conceived and initiated by Dr. David Teutsch, the director of the Center for Jewish Ethics at the Reconstructionist Rabbinical College (RRC). I am appreciative of his invitation to me to work on the life-cycle volume, and I continue to value his advice, input and suggestions. This is an appropriate place to call attention to Dr. Teutsch's publication *A Guide to Jewish Practice: Bioethics,* in which many ethical and medical issues related to sexuality and conception—including contraception, infertility, assisted reproduction, genetic testing and abortion—are discussed in detail.

Many people gave generously of their time to read early drafts, and I want to acknowledge their helpful suggestions, critiques and insights, all of which have improved this volume. I thank Rabbis Leah Richman, Nina Mandel and Myriam Klotz for thoughtful readings and comments. Rabbi Kevin Bernstein, who is a certified *mohel,* gave generously of his time, wisdom and experience in helping strengthen the section on *brit mila.* Dr. Simcha Raphael, Lawrence Bush, and Rabbis Linda Potemken, Sonya Starr and Ilyse Kramer provided sensitive guidance regarding issues of adoption. I want to acknowledge as well the RRC students with whom I have studied, debated and discussed issues of Jewish identity throughout the life-cycle, who responded to early versions of this material with sensitivity and creativity.

I want to offer special appreciation to Rabbi Sandy Eisenberg Sasso, whose 1977 booklet *Call Them Builders: A Resource Booklet about Jewish Attitudes and Practices on Birth and Family Life* was the first contemporary effort to apply Reconstructionist principles to many of the issues discussed in *Welcoming Children.*

Each volume of the *Guide* benefits from the diligence and dedication of the members of the Advisory Committee (see page vii), and I thank them for repeated readings both of the main text and the commentaries. The commentators (see page vii) have enriched the text with their insights, advice and observations. In addition to the time each took to write, they also offered helpful editorial suggestions on the main text.

Sharon Presser at the Reconstructionist Rabbinical Association and Cheryl Plumly at the Reconstructionist Rabbinical College helped prepare the manuscript and provided essential administrative support. I thank Marilyn Silverstein for her expert copy-editing, compiling the index and suggesting revisions of difficult passages.

The Jewish Reconstructionist Federation and the Reconstructionist Rabbinical Association kindly gave permission to use selections from, respectively, the *Kol Haneshamah* prayerbook series and the *Reconstructionist Rabbi's Manual.*

Finally, my thanks to the Center for Jewish Ethics at the Reconstructionist Rabbinical College for undertaking the publication of *A Guide to Jewish Practice.*

Richard Hirsh

February 2008 / Adar I 5768

WELCOMING CHILDREN

Introduction

Few moments in human life carry as much meaning as those that touch on the boundaries of life. Jewish rituals and observances can help guide us through such moments. Jewish traditions, values and customs can provide meaning and structure, and create opportunities to express many of the deepest feelings and highest hopes we experience when a child is born or adopted.

This book provides a guide to Jewish practice from a Reconstructionist perspective with regard to the arrival of children. It includes information, advice and guidelines for navigating through Jewish tradition as well as presenting contemporary innovations and options. A guide is not a code; it does not prescribe what each individual should do. A guide is a pathway through Jewish tradition that provides explanations, illuminates values and suggests approaches that are responsive to the needs of contemporary Jews.

A Reconstructionist guide reflects two fundamental commitments:

» *Respect* for the customs and traditions of the Jewish people, since each generation of Jews is the custodian of Judaism and bears the responsibility of ensuring its preservation and transmission; and

» *Responsiveness* to the needs of contemporary Jews, reflected in a willingness to adapt and innovate.

This book therefore strives to represent the broad outlines of traditional Jewish practices relating to the arrival of children while also suggesting departures from, changes in, or alternatives to some of those practices. Reconstructionist Judaism approaches tradition with the understanding that it needs to be interpreted and applied in response to contemporary circumstances.

Traditional Jewish discussions of welcoming children assume a husband/wife model of family. In many parts of the contemporary Jewish community however, a variety of other models of family—such as single parents, same-gender couples and blended families—have become common.

This guide to Jewish practice strives to be inclusive of the many models of "family," and sensitive to a variety of approaches to the roles and meanings associated with the word "parent." To reference single as well as partnered parents, wherever appropriate, this book uses "parent/s." (To avoid having the text become cumbersome and awkward, verbs are standardized to the plural: e.g., "parent/s are committed to. . . ." not "parent/s is/are committed to. . . .")

In the spirit of Mordecai Kaplan's self-conscious approach to innovation and adaptation, the guide addresses the changing world of American Jews in the 21st century with a desire to preserve individual personhood and collective peoplehood.

—D.D.M.

To the degree possible within the confines of clarity, this text tries to accommodate both biological and adoptive parents under the rubric "arrival of children." However, where issues specific to a category arise, they are treated independently, as in, for example, the discussion regarding adoption.

Prologue: "Identity," "Status" and "Descent"

Given the diverse nature of the contemporary Jewish community, the arrival of children sometimes raises questions of Jewish identity. It is helpful to make a distinction between the terms "identity" and "status." In this book, "identity" is used primarily to mean the ways in which individuals choose to identify themselves (for example, "I am Jewish"). In the case of a new child, it is the way in which parent/s identify the child, as in "my/our child is Jewish."

"Status" is used here to denote or deny affirmation of someone's "identity" by a community, group, people or some other form of collectivity. For example: "In our congregation, we recognize you as being Jewish," or "In our movement, your child is recognized as being Jewish." Conversely, "in our community" (or "according to *halakha* [Jewish law]"), we do not accept your claim of Jewish identity," or "We do not recognize your child as Jewish."

The Jewish psychologist Eric Erickson popularized the concept of "identity" after World War II. His writing on *Identity and the Life Cycle* awakened Americans to characteristic attributes of identity and corresponding tasks of identity formation facing individuals at each stage of life. —D.D.M.

When Jewish identity was passed through the mother only (matrilineal), and the Jewish community was primarily endogamous (in-married), "identity" and "status" were generally the same. In our contemporary Jewish community, this alignment can no longer be assumed.

Communities define themselves in part by determining who is and who is not a member. Communities cannot exist in a meaningful way without such determinations. Even when boundaries are low, permeable and soft, communities seek self-understanding through self-definition. Contemporary Jews have the responsibility as well as the right to establish definitions and understandings of what comprises Jewish identity and status because of the responsibility to preserve and to perpetuate the Jewish tradition. This is not meant as a way of judging people or of "keeping the gates closed." It is, rather, an attempt to understand Jewish identity as both substantial and significant by defining—as well as a community can in a time of transition—what it sees as the essential symbols of identity and the basic content of that identity.

Jewish identity and status are not determined on a purely individual or autonomous basis. Each of the contemporary Jewish religious movements, through their rabbis, congregations and central organizations, strives to establish basic positions and policies regarding Jewish identity that can be assumed to be consistent within the movement.

Traditionally, the arrival of a child in a Jewish family almost always meant the birth of a child to a Jewish woman married to a Jewish man. Since the first century of the Common Era until recently, the Jewish identity of a child has been determined by the Jewish identity of the mother ("matrilineal descent") or by the conversion of a child born to a non-Jewish mother (presumably but not necessarily) married to a Jewish man, or the conversion of an adopted child whose biological mother was not Jewish.

Within Reform Judaism (informally since 1949, officially since 1983) and Reconstructionist Judaism (since 1968, reconfirmed in 1979 and 1985), Jewish identity can also be established on the basis of having one Jewish parent, regardless of whether that parent is the father or the mother. Often incorrectly referred to as "patrilineal descent," these positions are more appropriately referenced as "ambilineal descent," since "patrilineal descent" suggests children are Jewish if and only if the father is Jewish.

"Patrilineal descent" and "matrilineal descent" are terms that reflect heterosexual, pre-modern norms as well as attitudes of much of modern Judaism. In light of the inclusion of gay and lesbian families and individuals into the progressive Jewish community, the discussion in this chapter assumes no distinction between heterosexual and same-sex parent/s. The term "ambilineal descent" is used as an inclusive referent that could accommodate heterosexual, gay or lesbian couples.

Both Reconstructionist and Reform Judaism endorse as minimal criteria for ambilineal Jewish identity that the child be born to parents at least one of whom is Jewish,

Horace Kallen, the American Jewish philosopher who coined the term "cultural pluralism," wrote that you could change your name and religion, but you couldn't "change your grandfather." —D.D.M.

and that the child be raised with an exclusively Jewish *religious* identity. (A Jewish child can have more than one *ethnic* identity, as might be the case, for example, of a Jewish child who is also African-American or Chinese.) Beyond this minimalist position is the desire that the child become educated in Judaism, engaged with Jewish ritual and spiritual life and socialized into the life of a Jewish community. For Jewish identity to be meaningful, it must have both rich content and a communal context.

Children recognized as Jewish by the liberal streams of Judaism may not be accorded the same status in the traditional movements. Even within the liberal streams, disagreement can occur in a particular case among rabbis or congregations associated with the same movement. (The same can be true in the more conservative movements that adhere to *halakha* as definitive.) It is helpful to discuss issues of Jewish identity with a rabbi.

Our hopes and expectations about behavior—education, worship, ritual life—that would help shape an active and meaningful Jewish identity, and not merely a passive one, apply equally, whether one or both parents are Jewish. —N.H.M.

Welcoming Children

The birth or adoption of a child is a powerful and profound moment in the life cycle. The arrival of a new life makes us acutely aware of the nearly limitless opportunities that life affords and of the miraculous potential that life places before us. As we become parents, we also become aware of the responsibilities that one generation has to the next, and of the central roles we play in shaping the identities of our children.

Children symbolize the continuity of the generations and create a change in status for the parent/s, a change in

As a parent who adopted her children as toddlers, I often wonder how we are to create a safe vessel in which to nurture their hearts and souls. Indeed, how does one go about carving out such a vessel? So much of our children's "selfhood" has already been created—as a beautiful tapestry to gaze in awe at, and appreciate, with each passing day. How do I learn to carry in my own hands these precious "selves"? How does one begin to tell a new story? "In the beginning," says the Torah—and so too, I begin to weave the Jewish stories into the fabric of their new lives as Jews. —I.K.

I remember vividly that my primary feeling when my wife first became pregnant was loss of control—the opposite of limitless opportunities. I hadn't realized until then that on some deep level, I had always believed that I was responsible for my fate and had the power to determine it. When things didn't go my way, I assumed that I had inadvertently affected the outcome. But expecting a child made me realize that we could not assure that our baby would be born healthy, nor would we have the power to protect her and raise her to be the person we wanted her to be. Truly, the imminent birth of our first child (and now decades of parenting) led me to a lifelong faith in the face of the unknown that I had never before experienced. —J.J.S.

role for spousal partners when there are two parents, and a realignment of relationships with one's own parent/s. Beyond the cognitive, relational, rational and psychological issues, however, there are powerfully primal emotions that rise within us in the presence of a new life.

Welcoming children is a common experience shared in all cultures, and there are many and varied ways in which cultural traditions create rituals to lend structure, order and meaning to this central moment and to the feelings it evokes. Religious traditions play a significant and often determinative role in how the arrival of a new life is understood within the community where the child's identity will be shaped and shared.

The Talmud (B.Talmud *Ta'anit* 23A) tells the story of Ḥoni the Circle Maker, who stopped to question a man planting a carob tree. When told that it would take seventy years for the tree to bear fruit, Ḥoni asked, "Are you certain that you will live another seventy years?" The man responded, "I found carob trees in the world that my ancestors planted for me, and so I too plant these for my children." Welcoming a child into the world provides a window through which to behold the cycle of the generations. Being granted the responsibility for the life of a new child—who does not yet have the power to care for himself or herself—invites us to experience our efforts in a larger light. —B.B.

When I became a grandmother, I recognized that I was reaping totally unexpected interest on a long-term investment. —D.D.M.

For many of us, our primary legacy to the world is our children. It is not just a question of genetic continuity. We know they will be repositories of our love and that they will be shaped by our values and the way we raise them. They carry into the future memories of us as well as some part of who we are. We become powerfully invested in our children because their lives increase the meaning of our own lives. —D.A.T.

The change in relationship affects all members of the family. When a sister becomes an aunt, or a nephew becomes a cousin, we expect different behavior and engagement from them vis-à-vis the new child. In some cases, this change is formalized in the role of "Godparent." —N.H.M.

One of the obligations—and opportunities—of parenthood is transmitting a religious heritage from one generation to the next. "You shall teach them [the words of Torah] to your children" (Deuteronomy 6:6) is a key commandment of the Torah. The transmission of the heritage of Judaism begins with the rituals and resources of tradition that celebrate and welcome a new child into the family and into the community of the Jewish people. Many of the emotions experienced at such a moment are connected to our having taken on the responsibility for forging new links in the chain of Jewish tradition.

We hope that if we raise our children in a rich, loving, textured Jewish environment and invest in excellent Jewish schooling and camping, they will receive our transmission. In fact, it does not always turn out that way. Our children are subject to many other influences. As parents, we are delighted to teach and share what is dear to us, with no guarantee that our best efforts will effect the desired outcome. —J.J.S.

The teachings of Torah can be understood in a broad sense to include any life-affirming values necessary to live a good life and build a better society. It is never too early to start instilling these values! This text is also instructing us to teach our children to love God with all of their hearts, souls and might. We want our children to increase the love in the world in any way they can, and it is our job to teach them how to do this by loving each other and ourselves as fully as possible. —A.B.W.

As babies grow into toddlers, we learn just how much we are constantly teaching them. Out of their mouths we hear words and phrases that we know to be our own, even when we do not remember saying them (or wish we could take them back!). In those moments, we become deeply aware of the effect of our words. Thus "You shall teach them. . . ." Whether intentionally or not we are constantly teaching words to our children. Let them indeed be words of Torah—of kindness, truth, and generosity. This is one of the many ways in which parenthood demands and inspires our commitment and attention. —B.B.

Rabbi Lawrence Kushner teaches "The job of a religious tradition is to give imagery, symbolism and grammar to experiences that finally transcend all language." (*God was in this Place and I, I did not know,* p. 168.) The presence of a new life is a microcosm of the mystery and meaning in creation itself. Our rituals, blessings and prayers strive to provide the "imagery, symbolism and grammar" to place the universal human experience of new life into the particular religious and cultural context of Jewish tradition.

The Concept of Covenant

Jews are part of the covenantal community of the Jewish people. As the Bible tells the story, the Jewish people is not a natural, geographic, ethnic or national people like some early contemporaries, such as the Egyptians, the Babylonians or the Canaanites. The story of the Jewish people begins instead with the Torah's depiction of God's call to Abraham to leave behind who he has been and embark on a journey toward a new identity that will be based on a covenantal relationship with God (see Genesis 12). By the time Moses is introduced in the second book of the Torah, the Israelite people have begun to emerge as a community, one whose identity will subsequently be confirmed through the acceptance of the Torah (see Exodus 19–20).

Being part of the Jewish people requires social connection. Peoplehood is a meaningless idea outside the context of community. Raising a Jewish child requires a communal context from the very beginning of a child's life, when the child's orientation to others starts to develop. —D.A.T.

The Torah describes the charge of God to Abraham as "Go forth from your land, from your place of birth, from your family . . . (Gen. 12:1). Parents who adopt might understand God's charge in this way:

Lekh l'kha: Go . . . with only your self (your person) and your name.
Meyartzekha: From your land . . . from your country and your birth parents and the orphanage in which you grew up.
Umimoladet'kha: From your place of birth . . . from your familiar language of origin, from familiar sounds and smells, from your home.
Umibeyt avikha: From your family . . . to trust in a new eternal family called the Jewish people, as you join us and become a "forever" child in our family and home. —I.K.

Since Judaism is both a culture and a religious tradition, defining Jewish identity is challenging. Throughout the generations of the Jewish people, the primary answer to the question of "*who* is a Jew" has been "one born into the Jewish people." This corresponds to the *ethnic/belonging* piece of Jewish identity. Another answer would be "one who converted to Judaism." The answer to the question "*what* is a Jew" has been "one who lives in covenant with God through the Torah tradition." This corresponds to the *religion/believing* piece of Jewish identity.

In North America, where terms such as "the Judeo-Christian tradition" and "Protestant, Catholic, Jew" are found, Judaism is often assumed to be a religious tradition along the lines of Christianity, where one is a member by affirmation of belief. But the aphorism that "one is *born* a Jew but one *becomes* a Christian" remains true; in Judaism, *belonging* comes before *behaving* and *believing*.

The rituals that accompany the entry of a child into the covenant of the Jewish people do not *confer* identity—they *confirm, consecrate and celebrate* identity. The function of the rituals for welcoming children is to create a spiritual-historical context within which the new child's status is announced, affirmed and celebrated.

Parents can provide the context and the roots of children's identity, but they must realize that children will grow into that identity in a unique way as they mature and learn more about themselves and the world. —A.B.W.

My wife Rachel raised the idea of reversing the order of the traditional *brit mila* ceremony, announcing our son's name before he underwent the circumcision. The ritual of *mila* affirmed and celebrated his identity and membership within the Jewish people, but by naming him first, we expressed the fact that he was *whole* just as he came into this world. (We made sure to discuss this with the *mohel* in advance.) —B.B.

P'ru Ur'vu: *Procreation as a Primary Value*

Jewish tradition has connected the blessing of children to the biblical commandment *p'ru ur'vu,* "be fertile and increase" (Genesis 1:28). Whether from a traditional or a progressive perspective, Judaism views procreation as a deep cultural value.

Among the blessings that children bring is the opportunity for parent/s to deepen their experience as human beings through fulfilling the responsibilities of parenthood. Children are also valued for the contributions we hope they will make to humanity and to the Jewish people and Jewish culture.

Rabbinic tradition, as embodied in the Talmud and, later, in Jewish codes, determined that having two children fulfilled the commandment to "be fertile and increase."

The Yiddish expression, *naḥas fun ḳinder,* expresses the special joy and pleasure that children can bestow on parents. —D.D.M.

Children are also valued simply for who they are. —A.B.W.

In addition to the blessings of parenthood, Judaism sees children as a blessing in themselves, new life to be celebrated. Children should be valued not only for what they might become but for who they are as inherently valuable human beings created in the image of God. They have an innate spirituality, souls with which they are endowed from birth. It becomes the obligation of family and community to provide the language to enable them to give expression to that spirit. —S.E.S

Some of the underlying understandings in these classical discussions contain positions that contemporary Jews might rethink in light of our egalitarian commitments. For example, according to classical *halakha,* the obligation to "be fertile and increase" is incumbent only upon men, but an egalitarian perspective would not distinguish between women and men with regard to that obligation.

As another example, talmudic authorities disagree as to whether having two sons or one son and one daughter fulfills the commandment to procreate. There is no classical opinion that two daughters would suffice, but an egalitarian perspective would not make a distinction between sons and daughters.

Issues of Jewish identity are sometimes raised in relation to assisted conception, including pregnancies that result from artificial insemination or egg donation. While the traditional imperative of *p'ru ur'vu* is not understood to require assisted conception, growing numbers of Jewish couples are utilizing assistance in reproduction. A rabbi can be consulted regarding issues of identity that arise when considering assisted reproduction.

If a woman or a couple chooses assisted reproduction and the sperm or egg donor is anonymous, according to many rabbinic authorities, there would be a preference for a non-Jewish donor, since that would reduce the possibility of a case of inadvertent incest. If the donor is known, the birth mother will presumably know the relationship boundaries between the families and will avoid selecting a donor where the issue of incest might arise. (For a further discussion of issues of assisted reproduction, see *A Guide to Jewish Practice: Bioethics* in this series.)

Not all contemporary Jews accept the imperative of procreation. Unlike some religions, Judaism has no tradition of celibacy. It recognizes sexuality as a blessing in itself, independent of procreation. Some Jews who decide to have children may choose to have no more than one child. Some Jews make the choice about how many children to have in the context of wider concerns about global overpopulation. Other Jews make such choices in the context of the importance of maintaining a vital and viable worldwide Jewish community. Health issues for one or both parents sometimes determine the number of children that a couple or an individual is able to have. Jewish women and Jewish men equally committed to careers as well as to committed relationships and to parenthood need to balance time, energy and resources, both material and personal. Any number of values and variables can go into the decision about whether to have children, and if so, how many to have.

Such decisions are intimate and personal. The presence of children is not a requirement for the creation of a Jewish family. There are Jews for whom biological conception is not possible. There are Jewish partners who voluntarily choose not to have children for personal reasons, or who may have raised children in an earlier marriage but choose

An additional factor to consider when deciding whether to become a parent is the opportunity for personal growth that parenting provides. Loving, nurturing, shaping character, disciplining and teaching are activities that shape the parent almost as much as the child. The continuity in the relationship gives us an opportunity to shape ourselves that is far greater than can be found in any other form of generativity. —D.A.T.

For most Jews the decision is highly personal, a choice made out of love and a deep desire to nurture new life. —S.E.S.

not to do so (or are no longer biologically able to do so) in a subsequent marriage.

Jewish tradition affirms the deeply personal rewards, blessings and opportunities of parenthood, and the importance for each generation to raise a new generation that can embody and carry forward the Jewish tradition. But it is also important to recognize that individuals have a right to choose whether to have children based on their specific circumstances, including their relationship with a partner or a spouse.

Those who choose not to become parents or who are unable to do so can contribute in a variety of ways to the transmission of Jewish tradition to the next generation. They might be teachers, mentors or tutors. They could host holiday celebrations and meals. They could attend synagogue services. By becoming involved in the life of a child, an adult can be an important, positive influence.

Unlike marriage, where divorce is possible, children are forever—parental responsibilities endure. —D.D.M.

The weight of the imperative to bear children remains heavy indeed. We may not realize it, but even when we affirm that people have the right to choose, our behavior often conveys a different message. We may assume that a childless couple *must* be trying unsuccessfully to conceive, or that it is clear to them that they would be happier as parents, or that they are postponing conception until a more opportune moment. Many people have yet to affirm non-parents as equally deserving of respect and admiration. —J.J.S.

As part of the preparation for becoming *bat/bar mitzva* in our community, youngsters are required to do oral history interviews with older members of the congregation. In this way, the generations of adults who do not regularly interact with the younger members develop mentoring relationships with the children. These are often deeply meaningful and long-lasting relationships that benefit everyone involved. —N.H.M.

Stepparents can be very central figures in the raising of a child or children in blended families. —M.K.

Jewish adults can also consider becoming foster parents. If a foster child is Jewish, then the foster parents can provide a Jewish context and experiences to support that identity. If a foster child is not Jewish, the foster parents can include her or him in their Jewish family observances.

The Jerusalem Talmud teaches that four questions will be asked of human beings when they reach the heavenly court upon their death. One of them asks *asakta bepriya ureviya?* Have you participated in the mitzva to be fruitful and multiply? Even if we cannot bear children or choose not to, this question can be understood in a myriad of ways: Did we raise children? Did we teach children? Did we listen to the voices of young people as seriously as those of adults? Have we shared our love and resources with children in our extended family and community? Have we concerned ourselves with the lives of children at risk? How have we ensured a world where future generations of children can grow and develop? The environmental slogan rings true—"We have not inherited the world from our parents. We borrow it from our children." —Y.R.

Veshinantam levanekha—"you shall teach your children" (Deuteronomy 6:7) is an instruction for each of us, whether children live in our homes or within our community. As mentors, role models and listening ears to our own or others' children, we can fulfill the role of being Jewish teachers. —B.R.P.

Close, loving, non-parental adults are critical to a child's life. They support the child and the parents in ways that are often not acknowledged in our society. It is appropriate to honor them in some way at the birth ritual. —A.B.W.

Conception, Pregnancy, Childbirth and Weaning

Beginning long before children arrive, significant moments can be enhanced through religious ritual, liturgy and blessings. Innovative Jewish rituals have been developed for such events as first learning of a pregnancy, marking the stages of a pregnancy, giving birth, seeing a child for the first time, nursing and weaning, among others. Jewish feminist scholarship has also helped to recover prayers and customs from earlier generations of Jewish women who found their own ways to mark these significant moments.

Because the range of innovative ritual is so wide, it is not possible to include references to all of the resources available for marking such moments. The bibliography lists several resources that can be consulted.

A number of Jewish customs and traditions associated with pregnancy and childbirth retain emotional power and psychological value. In contrast to the popular American custom of baby showers, one common Jewish practice is to refrain from having furniture, accessories and other items for a new baby delivered to the home until

An individual or couple who attempt to conceive a child with the help of technology (for example, artificial insemination or IVF) can use rituals and blessings that have been created to sanctify that process. —M.K.

after the baby has been born and viability has been established. In the tragic circumstance where a miscarriage, problematic delivery or post-partum complication results in the loss of the child, having to come home to a furnished baby room can be an intensely upsetting additional burden for the parent/s. Many Jewish families therefore make only essential preparations in the home before the birth, choosing to have accessories delivered afterward.

Many Jewish folk protection rituals and amulets were meant to protect the fetus and pregnant mother from the mythical Lilith in her demonic role as baby-snatcher. Close reading of the Lilith legends suggests suspicion and antipathy towards women who have never conceived or married. Today we can find ways of celebrating or ritually bracketing the liminal moments of the beginning of life without making others into villains. —N.H.M.

One value underlying the Jewish practice of avoiding baby showers is the caution against taking blessings for granted. Celebrating what has not yet happened distracts us from focusing on the blessings and challenges of the here and now. —J.J.S.

Medieval European folk beliefs in the power of evil spirits motivated the practice of deferring arrival of baby accessories. Its psychological wisdom survives today.

—D.D.M.

Some follow the custom of not disclosing the name of a baby boy until the *brit mila* ceremony (see next section). The origins of this practice may lie in folk beliefs based on the very real vulnerability of newborn children, especially in pre-modern times, when infant mortality rates were considerably higher. There may also be some distant connection to some of the underlying associations of circumcision (and blood) with protection (see, for example, Exodus 4:24–26, 12:13 and 12:23).

When our daughter was born, no one besides us knew her name until it was announced at her naming ceremony on the eighth day of her life. This was a very powerful as well as practical decision. We were able to spend several days with our daughter, getting to know her and using our budding relationship to help us decide on a name that truly fit her. We also chose a last name for our daughter (Weinmartin) that is a combination of her parents' last names (Weinberg/Martin). This was a decision to affirm our egalitarian values and the uniqueness of this new generation before us. By not announcing the name in advance, we avoided hearing people's reactions to the name—both positive and negative—that would have affected our decision-making process. —A.B.W.

Whatever the original intent of the custom to delay naming a child, it seems to fit with the sense that a newborn is somehow barely of this earth. We do not know the spiritual nature of the place from where the child emerged, but we know that it was categorically different than the world in which we dwell. I recall staring at our son during his first few days, overwhelmed by the task of having to choose a name for this angelic little being. None of the names we had considered seemed able to encapsulate him. By day six or seven, he had "descended" enough for us to choose. —B.B.

Delay in announcing a name perhaps served to delay bonding until viability was more clearly established. Today it is less common. Parents need not be fearful of sharing the name of the child before either a *brit mila* or a covenantal naming ceremony. I discourage this practice. We do not need to make parents more anxious than they already are. —S.E.S.

Because a *brit mila* would normally occur on the eighth day after birth, the delay in announcing the name would be minimal. If the baby is a girl, and the formal naming ceremony will not take place for some time, the custom of delaying the announcement of the name may become awkward as well as burdensome.

The Bible recounts a tradition of marking the weaning of a child with a celebratory meal (see Genesis 21:8). A number of contemporary rituals have been developed to mark this and other transitional moments in the relationship between parent/s and children (see pages 67–70).

Waiting until the day of the *brit mila* (or the naming ceremony for girls if held on the eighth day) to announce the name can also be a powerful way of ritualizing entrance into the community. There is intimacy in what parents call their children, and then there is the reality that the child will "make a name for him/herself" in the larger community as well. —Y.R.

Traditional practice had the father taking an *aliya* on the first Shabbat following the birth of a baby girl and having her named there with a *mishebeyrakh* prayer. The presence of the mother (and infant) was seen as unnecessary. In my own family lore, my Orthodox father took my mother in a cab to the hospital after candle lighting on Friday night (because she could ride for a health emergency), walked several miles home, and then realized that he had to walk back to find out if he had a daughter, because if I had been a girl, he would have had to name me in synagogue that morning! —J.J.S.

Parenting is filled with milestones. Almost every week of the first year of life is filled with new accomplishments for both child and parent. Many of these firsts get informally acknowledged and are perhaps even captured in a photograph. But it makes sense to acknowledge formally the incredible transitions continually being experienced by the parents as they learn to care for and continually let go of their evermore independent child. Weaning is the perfect metaphor for the primary job of parents: nourishing and releasing their children to be who they are. —A.B.W.

Circumcision

Brit Mila: *The Covenant of Circumcision*

According to the Bible, a symbol of the covenant that God made with Abraham is circumcision of male descendants on the eighth day after birth (see Genesis 17). This ritual is called *brit mila,* "the covenant of circumcision," with the emphasis on the covenant that the circumcision signifies. (The Yiddish term *bris* is also commonly used to refer to a *brit mila.*) *Brit mila* transforms an essentially surgical procedure into something with transcendent meaning. Understood from this perspective, a *brit mila* and a hospital circumcision are not equivalent events, although the surgical outcome is the same.

Brit mila does not "make" an infant boy Jewish. From a traditional point of view, if the birth mother is Jewish, an infant boy is Jewish at birth. The imperative of *brit mila* derives from the fact that the child is already Jewish; otherwise, there would be no obligation.

The decision to circumcise a son is often the first difficult decision a parent must make. It initiates parents into the demanding responsibilities of Jewish parenthood.

—D.D.M.

While Jewish law obligates the father to circumcise a son, in practice this responsibility is customarily fulfilled by arranging for a *mohel* (a male specialist in ritual circumcision) or a *mohelet* (a female specialist in ritual circumcision) to perform the procedure. In egalitarian and inclusive Jewish settings such as those in the Reconstructionist movement, the obligation to circumcise is shared by both Jewish parents, regardless of gender, or is assumed by a single Jewish parent.

The prayers and blessings that are part of a *brit mila* indicate the religious significance of the ritual. A chair is designated for the symbolic presence of the prophet Elijah, representing the hope for a messianic future in which peace and justice will prevail. Blessings are recited that link the commandment of *brit mila* to the covenant made with Abraham. Following the procedure, the Jewish name chosen for the child is publicly proclaimed for the first time. (For a detailed discussion of naming, see pages 44–51.) In many cases, the parent/s use this opportunity to explain the significance of the name and, if a child is being named after someone, to speak about that person.

Elijah is invoked at transitional times: at the end of Shabbat; when we give thanks for what we have eaten; at the *Pesaḥ* nexus between slavery and ultimate freedom; and when a new child enters our lives. At these liminal moments, we bind ourselves to past and future generations. In this moment, we hope to glimpse the promise of a world transformed through the eyes of this newborn. —B.R.P.

Providing an opportunity for parents and grandparents to express the emotions that accompany a birth can create a powerful moment. Remembering family members who have died but whose presence is felt is an important way of keeping the memory of the generations alive and linking new life with a rich past. Invoking those who are no longer present acknowledges the many influences that converge in the child. Often it is better to include these experiences before the actual circumcision, while the baby is still coddled by the parents. —S.E.S.

The traditional liturgy for a *brit mila* is brief. While it has become customary in contemporary Jewish life to include additional readings, prayers, poems and/or songs at life cycle events, parent/s should consider carefully the advisability of doing so at a *brit mila* if that would lengthen the ceremony significantly. The distractions of the procedure, parental anxiety and the not-unusual fussing of the infant can diminish the significance of additional creative materials.

The counting toward the eighth day for *brit mila* begins with the day of birth. For example, for a child born on a Monday before sunset, the eighth day is the next Monday. (Jewish days are counted from sunset to sunset.) If birth occurs in proximity to sunset, a determination needs to be made as to which date is the "date of birth" on the Jewish calendar. Parent/s should consult with a rabbi when the date of birth on the Jewish calendar is unclear.

Jewish law requires that circumcision be delayed or even deferred if there are significant medical risks involved. Health concerns override the requirement of *brit mila* on the eighth day. If there are any indications that the circumcision would potentially jeopardize the infant's health, the *brit mila* is delayed until medical authorities indicate it is safe to proceed.

Those planning a *brit mila* should keep in mind that some of the concerns about the ritual are precisely the ingredients that make the ritual so powerfully awesome. This can be a strong argument for keeping additions to the ritual to a minimum. —K.B.

Among the medical rationales for the eighth day are the residual immunities from the womb paired with the increased strength and vigor of the newborn. We can also consider the symbolic spiritual strength gained from having experienced six days of Creation and enjoyed a first Shabbat before entering the covenant on the eighth day. —B.R.P.

Brit mila as part of the conversion of an infant may be, but need not be, done on the eighth day. After healing has occurred, the conversion can be completed with immersion in a *mikveh*.

Because *brit mila* must occur on the eighth day, it can be done on Shabbat, on any of the festivals of *Pesaḥ, Sukkot* and *Shavuot,* and on *Rosh Hashana* and *Yom Kippur*. There are specific customs and norms as well as adjustments for the holiday or for Shabbat that apply under such circumstances; consult with a rabbi and with the *mohel/et*. If the *mohel/et* does not travel on Shabbat or holidays, additional arrangements may need to be made for accommodations within walking distance of where the *brit mila* will take place, and for the delivery of any necessary implements before Shabbat or a holiday.

Brit mila is customarily done in daylight hours, with a preference for earlier in the day. Tradition understands this as being meritorious because one is seen to be eager to fulfill a mitzva. An additional practical benefit is that guests and family may find it easier to attend earlier in the day. It is not unusual for the family to have some anxiety about the procedure, and scheduling the *brit mila* earlier in the day reduces the waiting time.

Many communities have more than one *mohel/et,* and rabbis as well as other parents can make recommendations. Many *mohalim* will be willing to meet in advance to

When *brit mila* falls on a Shabbat or holiday, it is usually done in the afternoon so that those who go to worship can then come to the *brit*. —D.A.T.

Some families choose to have weekday ceremonies in the afternoon when more family and friends are able to leave work and attend. —S.E.S

discuss the ritual and procedures and to answer any questions. When a due date is approaching, it is prudent to inform the *mohel/et* you intend to use; since *brit mila* is supposed to occur on the eighth day, and since neither parent/s nor *mohalim* can usually know in advance the exact date of the birth, scheduling is necessarily done with little advance notice and can require some juggling of times by the *mohel/et* to accommodate families.

It is customary but not required for there to be a *minyan* (prayer quorum of ten Jews over the age of *bar/bat mitzva*) present for a *brit mila*. While it is customary to invite family and friends to a *brit mila,* some people choose to hold a more private ceremony with only a few immediate family members and/or friends present. This may be followed by a larger celebratory gathering sometime later.

In areas distant from urban centers, the nearest *mohel/et* is sometimes several hours away. Early outreach to a *mohel/et* is recommended even if it is not certain that his or her services will be needed. In these cases a rabbi can be contacted to help make plans well before delivery. —N.H.M.

The week between birth and *brit mila* can be one of the most intense, exhausting, anxiety-filled and distracting weeks in young parents' lives, especially with a first child. There are benefits in accomplishing as much prior planning as possible. —K.B.

Having a large gathering in conjunction with the *brit mila* or naming places the child in the community where the child will be raised. While of course non-Jewish family members and friends ought to be included, this is an important opportunity for new parents to ask who will constitute the child's Jewish community. —D.A.T.

The goal of welcoming the child in the presence of a *minyan* reminds parents that the community supports them in raising and teaching their children. We raise our children in the hope that they will eventually feel called to serve the community in turn. —B.R.P.

One custom is to announce the *brit,* rather than to invite people to attend. What is the difference? One must either accept or decline an invitation, while one need not decline an announcement. Helping to create the community that witnesses a *brit* and being present to help the family celebrate are among the important reasons to attend. —B.R.P.

Brit mila often takes place at home, although some families choose to use a synagogue or other facility. Because it is a celebration as well as a consecration, the tradition of a *se'udat mitzva* (a sharing of food in celebration) is usually observed. This customarily follows the *brit mila,* but can occur some time later as well. Friends and other family members can help the family by offering to make arrangements for the *se'uda.*

While the primary participants in a *brit mila* are the parent/s and the baby boy, there are three traditional honorary roles that can be offered to relatives or friends: the *kvatter* and *kvatterin* (godparents) and the *sandek,* who stands by or holds the child during the procedure. The godparents have the honor of bringing the child into the room in which the *brit mila* will take place. While godparents do not play a significant role in Judaism, and the role at a *brit mila* is primarily honorary, traditionally they are viewed as guarantors that the Jewish education of the child will continue as he grows.

If the *brit mila* involves a small gathering at home, families sometimes choose to do a more public celebration on Shabbat in the synagogue, at which time the rabbi will call the parents and the infant to the *bima* at Shabbat evening services or for an *aliya* on Shabbat morning for a brief blessing or ceremony. —S.E.S.

Intermarried families may welcome the opportunity to invite non-Jewish family members to serve as godparents. —D.D.M.

Some *mohalim* prefer to have the child held by the person designated by the family as the *sandek,* as is customary. Others prefer to have the child placed on a special platform designed to keep him from moving around. While it is considered an honor to be invited to be a *sandek,* those extending the invitation and those considering it should be certain that the honoree will be able to fulfill the responsibility of holding the child or sitting alongside the child during the procedure.

The origin and literal meaning of the term *sandek* are obscure, but it is often said to be derived from Greek words meaning either "companion of child" or "patron of child." Many Jews today seem not to appreciate the traditional perspective of how great an honor it is to serve as the *sandek*. So important is the role that it has been likened to that of a *Kohen* performing Temple service, and at least one *responsum* holds that a *mohel* who wishes to act as the *sandek* for his son may be excused on that basis from what would otherwise be the father's obligation to perform the circumcision himself. —D.G.C.

Whether holding the baby or simply sitting alongside him, the *sandek* can be viewed as a type of guardian. He or she may choose to recite a particular psalm or set of biblical verses, or sing a certain song that speaks of safety and comfort. In any case, the *sandek* is called upon to give full attention to the child as he goes through this ritual. Whether hearkening back to an era in which *brit mila* was potentially dangerous or connecting to the spiritual significance of this transitional moment, the *sandek* plays a vital role in the life of this eight-day-old boy. —B.B.

The actual procedure for removing the foreskin takes but a few moments, and is followed by the naming ritual that is part of the *brit mila*. *Mohalim* will instruct the parent/s on appropriate hygienic and other care for the healing of the circumcision.

Hospital Circumcision

Because circumcision is a common procedure in North American culture, it is often available in the hospital following delivery. But because *brit mila* is a religious ritual in which the circumcision is secondary to the covenantal

Although the family and friends gathered for the ceremony are standing close enough to experience the drama of the circumcision, the parents, *mohel/et*, or designated guest should ask that people refrain from photographing the moment of the ritual itself. —Y.R.

Parents and other family members often suppress their anxiety about circumcision because they are eager to carry on tradition and welcome the baby boy into the covenantal community. Repressed feelings, however, have their own potency, and stressed fathers and grandfathers (and *sandeks*) may need to be attended to for signs of fainting or other physical symptoms. Women usually react less somatically, but not always. —J.J.S.

Circumcision is a common, simple procedure and the *mohel/et* is a well qualified professional who cares for the baby's well-being. —S.E.S.

On more than one occasion I have been asked, "What do we do with the foreskin?" The *mohel/et* is prepared to dispose appropriately of the foreskin, which in keeping with Jewish practice regarding the sanctity of the body usually involves burial. The foreskin can also be given to the parents to be planted with a new tree in honor of the child. One explanation for this ritual is that the tree planted at birth can provide the branches for the boy's *ḥupa* someday. —N.H.M.

content signified by the procedure, a routine hospital circumcision is not an alternative to *brit mila* as a religious ceremony. A hospital circumcision is a surgical procedure that has no religious meaning attached to it. In addition, a hospital circumcision normally occurs before the eighth day, whereas the *brit mila* is supposed to take place on the eighth day.

Hospital circumcision usually occurs without the parent/s present, in the absence of a community of family and friends, and without any blessings, prayers or other rituals that provide the context and content of *brit mila.* The surgical procedure for circumcision is usually similar to that of *brit mila,* although in certain hospital settings it may be done differently.

In contrast, the traditional observance of *brit mila* places the child in the warmth and care of the family and the family's community. Coming on the eighth day, *brit mila* occurs after the family has shared the first cycle of a week, including the first Shabbat together. Occurring most often in the home, *brit mila* is also a consecration of the family. The prayers that accompany the procedure add spiritual significance, and the sacred moment of bestowing a Jewish name is integrated into the ritual. A child is confirmed publicly as a member of the Jewish community.

Despite the arguments in favor of *brit mila,* some parents may decide on a hospital circumcision and then request that a rabbi come to add some or all of the prayers usually recited at a *brit mila,* including the naming of the child. While respecting such decisions, many Reconstructionist rabbis make a distinction between choice and need.

When a *mohel/et* is available in the community, or can be brought to a community, many rabbis will decline to officiate at a hospital circumcision before the eighth day, advocating instead that a *brit mila* be done.

If, as is sometimes the case, there is no *mohel/et* and circumstances do not allow for one to be brought to the community, it may be necessary to use the services of a doctor. Since the obligation of *brit mila* is on the Jewish parent/s and a Jewish ritual obligation can be fulfilled only by someone Jewish, in such circumstances it is preferable to have a Jewish doctor perform the circumcision, on the eighth day when possible. But since a hospital circumcision that is not done on the eighth day falls outside the traditional understanding of *brit mila,* whether the doctor is Jewish is no longer a factor. When a hospital circumcision is the only choice, parent/s may want a rabbi to be present to preside over whatever form of Jewish ritual can be added to a circumcision in such a setting.

Jewish law, however, does not recognize a hospital circumcision as fulfilling the requirements of *brit mila.* When a hospital circumcision has been performed, Conservative or Orthodox authorities would normally then require a subsequent procedure known as *hatafat dam brit,* in which a drop of blood is taken. In most Reconstructionist and Reform communities, authorities might suggest although not require the subsequent procedure, and would accept

Often Jewish doctors who perform ritual circumcisions join with a rabbi to do a *brit mila* at home. —S.E.S.

the hospital circumcision after the fact (*b'diyavad*). Older children and their parents should be informed about *hatafat dam brit,* which is a minor procedure that can be done at some later point if there is reason to do so.

Questioning Circumcision

From time to time, objections to the practice of circumcision are raised, sometimes by parent/s who are committed to raising their children as Jews but who object to *brit mila.* From a traditional point of view, *brit mila* is an obligation that is clearly and firmly rooted in the Torah and endorsed in later Jewish law. From a literary/legendary point of view, the *midrash* often identifies *brit mila* as one of the key guarantors of Jewish identity and continuity.

From a historical point of view, *brit mila* is an observance for which Jews took exceptionally high risks in many periods of persecution. And from a contemporary point of view, it is notable that all streams of contemporary Judaism—from traditional to liberal—continue to endorse the observance of *brit mila* as a covenantal rite.

In spite of where our imaginations may take us, experienced *mohalim*—and more convincingly, individuals who have experienced the procedure—rarely notice any physical discomfort from the *hatafat dam brit* procedure. *Mohalim* and rabbis should make this clear to parents, as well as to adults considering *hatafat dam brit.* Because social awkwardness is by far the greater challenge, it may make sense to delay the procedure until the child can completely understand the procedure and not experience confusion about the procedure and the reasons for it. —K.B.

For Jews who view the Torah and later *halakha* as humanly created and not divinely revealed, affirming *brit mila* simply as one of God's commandments is not compelling. Midrashic traditions are engaging as literature and suggestive in substance, but are unlikely to convince someone skeptical about the practice.

Brit mila is a powerful symbolic act around which strong feelings often emerge. Because Jews have placed such a high value on maintaining covenantal circumcision, choosing to disregard it has more significance than the non-observance of many other Jewish traditions. There is a strong emotional impact to being part of a line of tradition and continuity, which for many Jews is an important factor in maintaining the observance of *brit mila*.

Medical opinion about the value of circumcision is sometimes brought to bear in support of the practice, and studies can be cited that associate circumcision with a reduced risk of contracting certain conditions or diseases. While such studies may support the practice of circumcision, a Jewish endorsement of *brit mila* would not ultimately rely on its being medically advantageous, any more than endorsement of the traditions of *kashrut* would be

As increasing numbers of North American parents choose to forego circumcision of their sons, circumcision through *brit mila* becomes a more distinctly Jewish act. At a *bris,* we invoke the spirits of our ancestors—their joys and their sorrows—who have performed this ritual over the generations. We invite them to be with us, and with this baby boy, in that moment. —B.B.

contingent on the alleged health benefits of kosher food. (If a practice were to be definitively demonstrated to be harmful, that would be a different situation, since Jewish tradition is careful not to require practices that are clearly dangerous.)

Brit mila does involve a minor surgical procedure. There is a legitimate and understandable parental concern about causing pain to a child, something parents experience when, for example, they allow a child to receive necessary inoculations. While we cannot know what sensations an infant is able to experience by the eighth day of life, parents understandably worry about their child experiencing pain.

To reduce the possibility of pain or discomfort for the baby, most *mohalim* now use some form of mild anesthesia—often a spray applied both before and after the procedure. Following the procedure, the penis is immediately swabbed with an anesthetic antibiotic cream. The sensation the baby experiences may be similar to that experienced by an adult when cut by a very sharp object—a pain

Being a parent means that there will be times when we unintentionally hurt or disappoint our children. We take all kinds of actions on their behalf until they are ready to take responsibility for their own lives. Some of our most difficult experiences are often also those that carry great significance. A challenge of *brit mila* is that as one consequence of our actions our child may experience pain, however briefly. We hope this will be among the few times that our child may know pain as a result of meaningful and important actions that as parents we feel we must take. —Y.R.

that can be alleviated by applying pressure, although some temporary discomfort may remain for a short while.

Despite these concerns, several factors argue for maintaining the practice of *brit mila*—the centrality of *brit mila* in Jewish tradition, the endorsement of *brit mila* by all streams of contemporary Judaism, and the awareness that on a folk level, *brit mila* (even if interpreted as simple circumcision) remains a practice affirmed by most Jews. Ultimately, *brit mila* is a symbol of the communal and covenantal nature of Jewish identity. *Brit mila* is a tradition that reminds us that being a Jew means being a part of the Jewish people, not standing on one's own apart from the Jewish people.

Parents sometimes experience ambivalence about *brit mila.* They may, for example, need to navigate the tension between a commitment to Jewish tradition and a devotion to natural childbirth and child rearing. Trying to reconcile such concerns is the complex yet holy work to which Reconstructionist Judaism is committed. If you find yourself in such a position, you are not alone. Seek out fellowship and support from the Jewish community in approaching this conflict. A rabbi can be a vital resource. —B.B.

From the moment of birth or adoption, being a parent is an experience of learning to let go. With *brit mila,* we accept the inevitability of giving our children over to the frightening, satisfying, frustrating and, we hope, joyful events that will shape their *neshamot*—their character and their essence. —B.R.P.

Covenantal Ceremonies for Girls

Issues of Gender, Exclusion and Inclusion

Jewish tradition often made hierarchical distinctions between women and men with regard to ritual roles, obligations and opportunities, and did not always equally recognize or celebrate significant moments in the life of Jewish women. In contrast, contemporary liberal Jews have embraced egalitarianism, offering Jewish women equal access to the resources of Judaism and creating new rituals for important moments in their lives.

In approaching the life-cycle moment of welcoming a child, however, it is difficult to ignore the gendered assumption of *brit mila* as "the symbol of the Jewish covenant." For many progressive Jews, the notion of "*brit mila* equals Jewish" is problematic. Two primary concerns are the symbolic assumption that "Jewish equals male," and the fact that *brit mila* is obviously not a ritual that can be used to welcome Jewish girls into the covenant of the Jewish people.

Often, in traditional Jewish communities, a baby girl is welcomed by having the father take an *aliya* (the recitation of the blessings over one of the sections of the scriptural reading) during a Torah reading during a synagogue service. At that time, a blessing is offered in which the girl's Jewish name is announced. That the mother and the daughter are often absent in such a scenario only underscores the ritual disparity the tradition presents between marking the arrival of a boy versus the arrival of a girl. In many contemporary Jewish communities, there has been an understandable desire to go beyond such minimal offerings of Jewish tradition, and to create significant and meaningful ceremonies for a new daughter that are as significant as the rituals surrounding the welcoming of a son.

Many of the concepts and values associated with welcoming a baby boy apply to the welcoming of a baby girl. The communal and covenantal nature of Jewish identity indicates that a public welcoming of a daughter is equally significant to the welcoming of a son. The proclaiming of her Jewish name within a community that shares in the celebration of her arrival is an important public moment when Jewish identity is affirmed, and a covenantal welcoming ritual can represent continuity with earlier generations of Jewish women.

As with other new rituals created to celebrate significant moments in the lives of Jewish girls or women, opinions differ regarding the degree to which such ceremonies should simply be adaptations of the traditional rituals surrounding the welcoming of a son. For example, should a naming ceremony for a daughter take place on the eighth day after birth, as a *brit mila* would for a son? To do so

A more elaborate Sephardic ritual accompanies the naming of a girl, although it does not include a covenantal component. —S.E.S.

could be understood to affirm the equality of Jewish girls and boys within the covenant of the Jewish people. Or, should a naming ceremony for a daughter specifically not take place on the eighth day, to emphasize that the male experience need not be the norm, and to affirm that the female experience is unique? Parent/s may want to consider such issues and discuss them with a rabbi when planning a welcoming/naming ceremony for a daughter.

Celebrating a daughter's entrance to the community of Israel on the eighth day need not indicate that the ritual for bringing boys into the covenant of Israel is the norm. Boys and girls are different, but celebrating on the eighth day emphasizes the notion of covenant-making in the Jewish tradition. What other life-cycle rituals have their exact timing linked all the way back to our biblical ancestors and their search for a covenantal relationship with God? —Y.R.

The flexibility of choosing an appropriate date for welcoming baby girls allows us the possibility to recover from a birth, to plan a ceremony, and to offer guests more lead-time. With that in mind, celebrating the arrival of a daughter at *Rosh Ḥodesh*, or after a lunar month has passed, connects girls to the distinctly female cycles of the moon ensconced in our tradition. The midrash teaches that *Rosh Ḥodesh* was given exclusively for women to celebrate and to rest. Many Jewish women follow the tradition of immersing in the *mikveh* following their monthly cycle, a ritual whose rhythm mimics the phases of the moon. Several ceremonies for welcoming children use water, drawing on this ancient connection between women, the lunar cycle, and the renewal that comes each month which may be signified by the waters of the *mikveh*. —B.R.P.

One option for timing of a covenant ritual for a girl is to coordinate the ceremony with the cycle of the moon. Either new moon or full moon, whichever is closest to the birth, can be a meaningful moment at which to celebrate the welcoming of a baby girl. —B.B.

Because of the geographic dispersion of many families, when there is a celebration such as a *bar mitzva* or *bat mitzva* service that brings people together at a time near the arrival of a new child, some parent/s may want to consider having a welcoming/naming ceremony in the context of that service. However, it should be noted that Jewish tradition generally discourages "mixing of *simḥas*," diluting the celebration of one event by placing another one in the same moment. Such options should be carefully considered. —R.H.

Rituals of Welcoming and Naming

The arrival of a daughter is as important as the arrival of a son. The embrace of egalitarianism in contemporary progressive Jewish communities has led to the development of many new ceremonies, rituals and liturgies for welcoming Jewish girls into the covenant of the Jewish people. Some of these have become standardized in various rabbinic manuals, in Jewish home prayer books and other collections of liturgical materials, and in volumes devoted to Jewish feminism. Many are also now available on the Internet (see, for example, *www.ritualwell.org*). In addition to these more formal collections of ceremonies, many parent/s have created new forms of welcoming and innovative naming rituals, sometimes blending pieces of various ceremonies into a unique ceremony. Unlike *brit mila,* no one basic ritual for welcoming girls has yet emerged.

New ceremonies for welcoming girls into the covenant usually include both recitations and rituals. One popular practice is to have a naming ceremony in the context of a Shabbat service, since Shabbat is also considered to be a sign of the covenant. In such rituals, blessings are recited, the Jewish name of the child is announced, and the parent/s speak about the person/s for whom the child is named, as well as about their own hopes and dreams for their new daughter.

Various other rituals using Jewish symbols and traditions have been developed—some designed to be carried out in the home, others in the synagogue. Among those that have been developed are: a foot-washing ritual, a tree-planting ritual, an immersion in a mini-*mikveh* (ritual pool), a candle-lighting ritual, a ritual that uses the symbols of the *havdala* ceremony at the end of Shabbat, or a *talit*-wrapping ritual. In such ceremonies, blessings and remarks as well as the naming are usually included.

Families may choose from among the many rituals that have been created for welcoming a daughter, or they may want to combine pieces of different rituals into a unique ceremony. They may also want to consider creating a new ritual and/or a set of blessings to use for a welcoming ceremony. The absence of a fixed covenantal ritual for girls offers an opportunity to be creative and innovative in shaping something that reflects the Jewish insights, ideas and symbols that are of particular value to a family. A rabbi can be a helpful resource in selecting and/or shaping a ritual of welcoming and naming.

Common to most rituals for girls is a blessing welcoming the daughter into the covenant of the Jewish people, and expressing the hope that as she has entered the covenant, so may she grow into a life of Torah, family joys and good deeds. To fashion something totally new loses the connection to any shared tradition, and sends the message that while there is something sacred and fixed that we do for a boy, for a girl we can do whatever we want. While allowing for creativity in covenantal ceremonies for girls (just as we do for boys), we should also ensure a core traditional component. —S.E.S.

When possible, I like to incorporate a *ḥupa* into the welcoming of new children—boys *and* girls. Couples often have a tallit or *ḥupa* that was used during their wedding ceremony. This can be held up over the couple and the child during the ritual to symbolize the expansion of the Jewish home they established at the wedding. —N.H.M.

Naming

Naming and Identity

Choosing a name is an important symbolic and spiritual decision. Names embody memories, hopes and ideals. The Jewish name announced at a naming ceremony or *brit mila* is the name that will be used when the child reaches the age of *bar* or *bat mitzva* and is called to the Torah; it is the name used on Jewish documents that sanctify committed relationships; it is the name used in the *mishebeyrakh* prayer for healing; and it is the name by which Jews are memorialized after death. Perhaps most importantly, when children are old enough to ask why they are named as they are, including for whom they are named, the answers that parents give become an essential piece of their developing identity.

At the time we adopted them, our children had been orphaned. We chose to retain our adopted children's first names that were given by their birth parents. Those names are the vessels that hold the key to their precious, difficult and complex past. We gave them middle and Hebrew names in the hope that a spiritual bridge would be created to connect their past to their present, and their present to their future. Like all children, their lives are a gift, in this case a gift they bring to the Jewish People. —I.K.

In *Judaism as a Civilization* (1934), Rabbi Mordecai Kaplan wrote:

> The matter of names is rarely included in a discussion of Judaism . . . [but] we cannot overlook the importance of names as a means of fostering Jewish consciousness. . . . The name that a person bears carries with it cultural implications and associations and identifies [him/her] with a particular civilization. (pp. 453–454)

The arrival of a child creates the opportunity of choosing a name. In Jewish tradition, as well as in feminist theory, great importance is attached to naming. Names give a tangible reality to people and to things. The act of naming represents both power (the authority to give the name) and relationship (the connection between parent/s and child that makes the name meaningful). The choice of a name for a new child is a matter of great importance, meaning and potential.

In earlier generations, when Jews were concerned primarily with adapting and integrating into American life, children were often given first names that had no ethnic, biblical or Hebraic associations. The choice of a name often reflected the desire to "fit in." Today, when North American Jews have successfully integrated into the larger communities in which they live, the choice of a name becomes an opportunity to reinforce and make central the Jewish identity of a child.

Jewish immigrants to the United States often took as first names the last names of famous British writers (e.g. Milton, Sidney) to Americanize Hebrew or Yiddish names such as Moshe (Moishe) or Shmuel. —D.D.M.

Choosing a Name

Jewish tradition has evolved a variety of *minhagim* (customs) regarding naming, many of which derive from the diverse cultures and communities of origin from which North American Jews are descended. While naming is primarily in the realm of custom, the old adage that "custom has the force of law" often proves true in individual family circumstances, where the choice of a name can provoke controversy as well as strengthen cohesion. Naming can become an issue through which various family dynamics are refracted, and competing concerns can often arise, such as when a choice perpetuates the name of one deceased relative instead of another.

Some basic customs can be considered. Naming a child after someone in the family is a widespread tradition. Jews of European or Russian descent (*Ashkenazim*) will generally name children after a deceased relative, while Jews descended from the Mediterranean communities (*Sefardim*) will often name after a living relative.

Some parent/s simply choose one (Jewish or Hebrew) name, such as *Shira* or *Nadav,* in which case the "English" name and the "Jewish" name are the same. Other parents

It is not always possible to predict the reaction of family members. We narrowly avoided a crisis when we told my mother that we planned to name our daughter after a sister of mine who had died as an infant long before I was born. I thought my mother would be moved that we were honoring her memory, as well as preserving the name of the ancestor for whom she had been named. Instead, my mother became very upset; that name preserved traumatic associations and that made it unlucky in her eyes. It is very important to check. —J.J.S.

choose an English name by which the child will be known within the larger culture, and then choose a "Jewish name" by which the child will be known in the sacred settings of the Jewish community. (A "Jewish name" can be a Hebrew, Yiddish or Ladino name, or some other Jewish cultural variant.)

Some parent/s choose the same English and Jewish names: For example, Benjamin and *Binyamin* are English and Hebrew equivalents, as are Rebecca and *Rivka*. Other parents choose an English name and a Jewish name that may not have (and need not have) anything in common: For example, Ellen in English and *Esther* in Hebrew. Still other parents choose English and Hebrew names that have the same meanings, even if derived from different languages: For example, the names Joy and *Simḥa* have the same meaning, despite being derived from different languages.

When the gender of the child and the person for whom s/he is being named are the same, the same name is often used. When the gender is different, it is often relatively easy to transpose the meaning of the name: A new son can be named *Ḥayim* after a female relative named *Ḥaya*, since both names derive from the same Hebrew root word meaning "life."

When parents want to name after someone who does not have a Jewish name (it is not unusual for someone Jewish not to have been given a Jewish name, or for one to

Name choices can also reflect the mix of ethnic identities found in many families, especially when adoptive children come from other countries. —N.H.M.

have been forgotten over time), and the meaning of that person's English name is known, a Hebrew equivalent can sometimes be suggested. For example, if naming after someone whose name was Rose, the Hebrew name *Shoshana* could be chosen.

Some families choose a name that begins with the same letter as the name of the person for whom the new child is being named. For example, the Hebrew name *Tova* can be used to honor the memory of someone named Tillie.

Another tradition is to choose a name that appears in the Torah reading corresponding to the week of the birth, or in another biblical reading that occurs in proximity, perhaps during a holiday. For example, a girl born during the week of the holiday of Purim might be named *Esther,* after the heroine of the story; a boy born during Hanuka might be named *Yehuda* (Judah), after one of the heroes of the Maccabean revolt. A child can be named for more than one person. Some families do this by giving different English and Hebrew names. Other families use a first and middle name.

Children can also be given a name that has symbolic meaning. Adopted boys, for example, are sometimes named Jonathan (Hebrew *Yonatan*) because the name means "God has given." Parent/s honoring the memory of family members who perished in the *Shoah* (the Holocaust) might choose the name Zachary (Hebrew *Zakharya,* meaning "God remembers").

Some parents may choose a Jewish name that is gender-neutral (such as *Yona* or *Simḥa*) out of a concern to avoid the gender stereotyping associated with "male" and "female" names.

Names of the Parent/s

In Jewish tradition, a child's Jewish name does not stand alone, but is linked to the names of the parent/s. When a Jewish person is called by name in "a matter of holiness" (*d'var shebikedusha*), she or he is called by the "Jewish name." When a child has two Jewish parents, the full Jewish name would follow this formula—the child's Jewish name, followed by *ben* ("son of") or *bat* ("daughter of"), followed by the father's Jewish name (the patronymic), followed by *v'* or *u'* signifying "and" in Hebrew, followed by the mother's Jewish name (the matronymic). As examples: *Yona bat Yosef v'Leah, David ben Yishai v'Rachel.* For same-sex Jewish-Jewish couples, the full name would include the names of both of the mothers or both of the fathers. As examples: *Miryam bat Naomi v'Sara*, *Ya'akov ben Sh'muel u'Moshe).* If a parent does not know her or his Jewish name, it might be found on a *ketuba* (wedding document).

If a Jewish parent does not have a Jewish name, the arrival of a child can be an opportunity to choose one. There is no formal ritual required for an adult Jew choosing a Jewish name, although some adults may want to

Naming ourselves can be a powerful way to mark an adult (re-)entry into Jewish life. Having a new child, by birth or adoption, may be an auspicious time to recognize one's own change in status. Immersion in a *mikveh* or another body of water is an ancient ritual for recognizing transitional moments in our lives and is increasingly used in a creative new ways—including welcoming children or taking on a Hebrew name. —B.R.P.

have some form of ritual or blessing in which a name is formally bestowed or affirmed.

For single parents, tradition sometimes suggested using the parent's name following *ben* or *bat* followed by the name of a grandparent of the opposite sex. Many single Jewish parents today would not feel the need to create a symbolic second parental name and would simply choose to name a child X, the son or daughter of Y.

Naming When One Parent Is Not Jewish

In traditional Jewish communities, the name of a non-Jewish parent is not normally used either as a matronymic or a patronymic. Some traditional communities follow the practice of using the name of a Jewish grandparent in conjunction with the name of the Jewish parent. Other com-

Omitting the name of a non-Jewish parent diminishes her or his role, and is neither welcoming on the part of the Jewish community nor encouraging to this parent to participate in the Jewish upbringing of the child. —S.E.S.

In a closed adoption, adoptive parents may know a child's birth mother is Jewish, but not have any information regarding the father's status. Or while the birth mother may be Jewish, the birth father may not be Jewish. In such cases, it makes sense (at least from a Reconstructionist perspective) that legal practice becomes replicated in Jewish practice. Just as the state re-issues a birth certificate indicating the child is "born" to the adoptive parents, similarly a child can be named *ben* or *bat* of adoptive father and mother. —S.R.

In the case of conversion, it is possible to honor the memory of a family member of the convert by giving a Hebrew name that is evocative of the name or character of that person even though he/she was not Jewish. —S.E.S.

Yet the decision to link one's name to that of one's child may be a step on the path of becoming a Jew. —D.D.M.

munities would use only the name of the Jewish parent. Some might use "Abraham" or "Sarah" in place of a non-Jewish parent's name, since they are considered the spiritual father and mother of the entire Jewish people.

Within the liberal Jewish community, where it is not unusual for intermarried couples to be raising Jewish children, other choices may be more appropriate—more reflective of the commitment of the non-Jewish parent and more respectful of the reality that the child does indeed have two parents. One easy alternative is simply to use the English name of the non-Jewish parent as the patronymic or matronymic, perhaps placing the Jewish name first (examples: *David ben Sara v'*Christopher or *Sara bat Raḥel v'* Christine).

Interfaith couples sometimes suggest giving a "Jewish name" to a non-Jewish parent. Most Reconstructionist rabbis would discourage this, even if it simply meant using a Hebrew equivalent of an English name (e.g., John becomes *Yoḥanan*), because it blurs the distinctions of religious identity for the parents, and may also convey an impression that the non-Jewish parent has converted to Judaism.

Adoption

Adoption in Jewish Tradition

Jewish tradition warmly and fully accepts adopted children, and adoption has become an increasingly significant part of contemporary Jewish life. However, adoption as understood in contemporary North American culture is not reflected in the classical Jewish legal codes. In civil adoption, the relationship between the adoptive parents and the child is legally recognized as replacing the lineal relationship that the child had with the birth mother (and father). In Jewish tradition, the lineal relationship between a child and the birth parent/s cannot be undone. Consequently, the concern of traditional Jewish authorities has primarily been the identity of the child in terms of her/his birth family.

When we remember that *halakha* (Jewish law) is essentially a tradition having to do with legal determinations, it is not surprising that such issues are of concern. Classical Jewish text sources often assumed in discussions of adoption that the birth mother was Jewish, and that the adoptive parents had entered the picture because of the inability of the birth mother to raise the child. Given the often disrupted patterns of Jewish communal life in the pre-modern period, the less-advanced state of medical knowledge and care, and economic, political and geographic factors it is not hard to imagine that within the Jewish community a family might take on the responsibility for raising a child not born into that family.

In such settings, the issue of Jewish identity would not be controversial: if the birth mother was Jewish, the child was Jewish. The types of questions that could then arise might include whether to use the adoptive father's name or the birth father's name as a patronymic, or whether, if the birth father was a *Kohen* or *Levi* (a descendent of a priestly family of ancient Israel), the child retained that status after adoption. Can ritual obligations that presume parenthood (for example, the *brit mila* of a son) be transferred to an adoptive family? Would an adoptive child be required to mourn adoptive parents and/or birth parents? These sorts of questions would not arise if the birth mother was known not to be Jewish.

In addition, Jewish law reflects concerns about legitimacy as well as accidental incest. The traditional category of *mamzer* (one born of a relationship prohibited by Jewish law) could potentially apply, since an adopted child could inadvertently enter into marriage with a prohibited relative, and any resulting children would then fall into that category.

As adoption became a more common experience in Jewish life, it became the preference in many traditional communities for a child adopted into a Jewish family not to have a Jewish birth mother, since that would eliminate just these sorts of halakhic questions. Despite such concerns, in some parts of the contemporary Orthodox Jewish community there remains a preference for adopting children of a Jewish birth mother so that children born Jewish do not end up being raised in another faith community.

Adoption and Conversion

Contemporary adoption proceeds from different sets of assumptions and circumstances than those found in traditional Jewish sources. The civil/legal assumptions about transfer of lineage from the birth family to the adoptive family often correlate with the emotional and psychological experience of the adoptive parent/s—that the child is "their child." Reciprocally, as many adopted children grow older, they experience their adoptive parents as "their parents."

The Jewish status of an adopted child with a non-Jewish birth mother is traditionally established by conversion of the child to Judaism. This requires immersion in a *mikveh* for boys and girls, and for boys, *brit mila l'shem gerut* (covenantal circumcision for the sake of conversion), or the taking of a supplementary drop of blood (*hatafat dam brit*) if the boy was circumcised before the time of adoption.

Many Jewish parent/s will therefore work with a rabbi to arrange for the conversion of the child. Since the visit to the *mikveh* should occur only when the child is old enough to manage the brief immersion, the steps in conversion of an infant or young child may be spread over a period of time. For example, a *brit mila* might occur very early on, with the *mikveh* following a few months later, and a public naming ceremony at yet another time. The naming can also be done at the time of the *mikveh*. (There may be legal issues involved regarding whether an adopted child can be converted, including whether circumcision is permitted, prior to finalization of the adoption procedures; parent/s should check with legal counsel and/or adoption agency staff.)

When a boy who is past infancy is adopted, circumcision may require a hospital setting. Some hospitals will allow a *mohel/et* to perform the procedure with requisite medical staff on hand. Since the *mohalim* certified by Reform Judaism's *brit mila* program are medical doctors, one of them may be available to perform the procedure in a hospital setting.

The older a boy is at the time of adoption, the more complex this procedure can become, and parents will want to consult with a rabbi and health-care professionals in evaluating the medical, psychological and emotional issues. While traditional Judaism mandates circumcision for conversion, liberal rabbis hold a range of positions, depending on the age of the child and the circumstances of the family.

Differences of Opinion

Many adoptive Jewish parents support the conversion of adopted children as an acknowledgment that families created through adoption are different from families created through childbirth. Conversion can be seen as a way of honoring the different journey to Jewish identity taken by the adopted child. Having a different journey does not mean having a less meaningful, legitimate or significant one. And conversion can be seen as a way of affirming the uniqueness of adopted children rather than denying that there is any difference between them and other children.

Within the Jewish adoptive community, however, there are differences of opinion about the traditional requirement of conversion. Some adoptive parent/s object to the expectation that an adopted child requires conversion in order to be accepted as Jewish. For other parents, particularly those who choose adoption as a consequence of infertility, requiring conversion may seem both hurtful and punitive. Some parents believe that requiring conversion suggests a concession to the most traditional part of the Jewish community. For other parents, conversion suggests that the child is not really theirs. Requiring conversion may also be seen as suggesting that ritual acts rather than the ongoing daily experience of Judaism in the family are determinative in the formation of a child's Jewish identity.

In Israel, conversions by any but Orthodox rabbis recognized by the state are often rejected when the convert applies for permission to marry. The legal authority of the Israeli rabbinate over conversions to Judaism influences debates over the legitimacy of liberal conversions in North America. —D.D.M.

Most Reconstructionist rabbis recommend the conversion of an adopted child for a number of reasons—the most powerful of these relating to issues of identity and status. If an adopted child had a non-Jewish birth mother, the conversion of the child ensures a wider circle of acceptance of the child's status as a Jew within the community. In affirming that adopted children should be converted, Reconstructionist rabbis are affirming their commitment to Jewish peoplehood and *klal Yisrael*. This reduces potential complications that can arise in adolescence or adulthood. Recognizing that adoption is a bonding process, a ceremony of conversion can result in a deepening of that experience. Conversion can also lend a spiritual and emotional dimension to what might otherwise be nothing more than a legal process. Many of the issues involved require sensitive, respectful and compassionate conversations between parent/s and a rabbi.

Jewish law holds that a child converted in infancy has the obligation to affirm (as well as the right to deny) the conversion when s/he reaches the age of majority (*bat* or *bar mitzva*). Some rabbis therefore recommend that some ritual of affirmation or of conversion take place before a *bat* or *bar mitzva* ceremony as a way of having the child confirm an earlier decision that had been made by her or his parent/s. Other rabbis would consider the *bat* or *bar mitzva* ceremony itself as a ritual of identity affirmation.

However, if an adopted child never had a formal conversion in infancy or early childhood, but has been raised with an exclusively Jewish religious identity, a Reconstructionist rabbi may suggest some ritual acts of affirmation, depending on the circumstances, the age of the child and other factors. Some Reconstructionist rabbis might require some formal rituals of conversion to confirm the Jewish status of the child. Most Reconstructionist rabbis would affirm such a person's adult Jewish status without requiring any formal ritual steps, although in individual cases a person might voluntarily choose some ritual of affirmation and/or formal conversion.

The conversion of an infant, who can neither understand the process nor consent to it, is problematic. The *Shulḥan Arukh* allows a *bet din* (rabbinical court) to perform the conversion of an infant (or an older minor) on the theory that becoming a Jew is a privilege (*zekhut*) for the child, and the *bet din* is literally doing the child a favor in converting him or her (*Yoreh De'ah* 268:7–8). Because an infant conversion is not "voluntary," the converted child has the right to annul the conversion upon attaining the age of *bat/bar mitzva*. If the right is exercised, the "ex-convert's" halakhic status becomes that of a non-Jew, rather than that of a Jewish apostate. The convert's right to annul the conversion is strictly limited in time, in that a convert who, after becoming a legal adult, acts in accordance with Jewish custom for even a very brief period is deemed to have ratified the conversion and cannot undo it. —D.G.C.

When an older child comes to the *mikveh* after being raised as a Jew, I acknowledge her or his identity by calling the immersion an "affirmation" rather than a conversion. Other affirmations may take place surrounding the bar/bat mitzva ceremony, when tradition suggests that adopted children assert their choice to enter the Jewish people, independent of their parents' wishes when they adopted the child. I am inclined to recommend rituals such as a spoken affirmation of Jewish commitment or immersion in a *mikveh* to all of our children, whether born Jewish or converted to Judaism. —B.R.P.

A fuller discussion will be featured in the forthcoming "Conversion" volume in *A Guide to Jewish Practice*. —R.H.

Adoption and Naming

When choosing a Jewish name for an adopted child, the question of what name/s to use as the patronymic and/or matronymic should be addressed. One traditional position holds that in the conversion of an adopted child—as in the conversion of an adult non-Jew—the appropriate patronymic and matronymic would be "Abraham" and "Sarah." In Hebrew, this would be rendered as *Avraham avinu v'Sara imenu* ("Abraham our father and Sarah our mother") to indicate a conversion, in contrast to someone born Jewish to Jewish parents whose names happen to be "Abraham" and "Sarah," where the words *avinu* and *imenu* would not be used.

In traditionally observant Jewish communities, some restrictions remain in effect regarding whether converts can marry people identified as *Kohanim* (from priestly families), and that is one reason why the use of *Avraham avinu v'Sara imenu* to indicate that someone came to her or his Jewish identity via conversion remains important. Since liberal Jewish communities do not recognize such marriage restrictions regarding converts, the maintenance of the tradition of using *Avraham avinu v'Sara imenu* is less compelling.

Contemporary circumstances, concern for the integrity of the family, and sensitivity to the feelings of the parent/s suggest that, despite the traditional position, it is appropriate for adopted children to have the names of the parents who are raising them, regardless of whether a conversion has taken place. There is warrant for this position in traditional sources as well, where a concern for embarrassment of the parents is seen as a factor mitigating the need to confirm whether a conversion occurred. Thus, in most Reconstructionist communities, adopted children would have added to their Jewish names the Jewish name/s of the parent/s who are raising them—for example, *Leah bat David v'Shulamit,* rather than *Leah bat Avraham avinu v'Sara imenu.*

Pidyon Haben: *Redemption of the Firstborn Son*

In traditional forms of Judaism that preserve the lineal distinctions among *Kohen* (a presumed descendent of the biblical Aaron, the first High Priest), *Levi* (a presumed descendent of the biblical tribe of Levi) and *Yisrael* (one descended from any other part of the Jewish people), there is a prescribed ritual called *pidyon haben,* "redemption of the firstborn son." (Since *Kohen* or *Levi* status is transmitted from fathers to sons, there was no parallel ritual for girls.)

Pidyon haben takes place on the thirty-first day after birth (unless it falls on Shabbat or a major holiday, in which case it occurs on the next day). This ritual grew out of ancient traditions of biblical Israel, where *Kohanim* and *Levi'im* were consecrated by birth to the service of God in the priestly "civil service" of the Jerusalem Temple in place of Israelite firstborn sons.

The Torah requires the exemption of a firstborn Israelite son from sacred service, but requires a ritual of exchange in which the child is "redeemed" for what appears to have been a contribution to the sacred shrine system. (Numbers 18:15–16)

The tradition of *pidyon haben* applies only when three conditions are met: The child must be delivered vaginally, not by Caesarean section, since *pidyon haben* applies only to a *peter reḥem* ("womb-splitter"); the child must be the firstborn of the mother (but need not be the firstborn of the father); and the father of the child must not be a *Kohen* or *Levi* himself, nor can the mother be the daughter of a *Kohen* or a *Levi* (*bat Kohen, bat Levi*), since descendents of *Kohen* or *Levi* families do not have to be "redeemed."

With the advent of the modern period, liberal forms of Judaism ceased to observe the distinctions among *Kohen, Levi* and *Yisrael* and, consequently, in Reconstructionist and Reform Judaism the traditional *pidyon haben* ceremony is rarely observed. In addition to rejecting the priestly presumptions and prerogatives of the ceremony, the non-egalitarian nature of the ritual runs counter to progressive Jewish principles. (While there is no traditional ritual for *pidyon habat* [redemption of the daughter], there have been some attempts within the traditional Jewish community to create some adaptation or variation of *pidyon haben* for daughters.)

We celebrated a *pidyon habat* for our first-born daughter, even after welcoming her in a *brit* ceremony. The *pidyon* was more intimate than the naming, and reminded us of our new responsibilities. Because the essential ritual of the *pidyon* symbolically represents "redeeming" children from service to God, the ceremony reminds us that we do not "own" our children's bodies or souls. —B.R.P.

While all children are unique and to be valued equally, the significance of the first child is distinctive. Although liberal Judaism may no longer recognize the priestly tribal divisions, there is psychological and emotional wisdom in the acknowledgment of the profound transformation that a first child creates in the family. The importance of continuing to acknowledge that transformation through ritual, symbol and prayer is worth considering. An adaptation of *pidyon haben* might dispense with some of the halakhic qualifications, for example, making no distinction between a vaginal birth and a Caesarean section. There could be an acknowledgment that a first-born child in a second marriage (even if the parent/s may have had children in a prior marriage) represents a transformation for the family, and that a ritual would be appropriate.

Such ceremonies devoted to consecrating the family and/or marking the arrival of a first child are often held on or about the thirty-first day after birth, around the same time as when a traditional *pidyon haben* ceremony would be held. Since the initial weeks following the arrival of a child are usually busy, some families prefer to take advantage of the initial month to allow for a more leisurely and relaxed ritual and/or celebration.

In 1977 the Reconstructionist movement published one of the first alternative *pidyon* ceremonies to celebrate the first child born to or adopted by a family. Called *Seder Kedushat Ḥaye Hamishpaḥa*—"A Ceremony of Consecration to Family Life," it was published in a booklet entitled *Call Them Builders.* Life's sacredness is sensed in a deeply personal way at the birth or adoption of a first child. Instead of "redeeming" the child, the ceremony calls for a dedication of the family to Jewish living and social responsibility. A gift of *tzedaḳa* is presented as a symbol of commitment to the values that the parents hope the child will emulate. —S.E.S.

Conclusion

As noted at the beginning of this discussion, few moments in the lifecycle are as powerful as the birth or adoption of a child. Many deep, primal and powerful feelings are stirred up, and Jewish tradition seeks to provide structure and content that can give meaning to this dramatic and celebratory moment. Religious traditions provide a context within which such moments can be understood.

When a new child comes into the Jewish community, the event transcends the family, becoming a part of the life of the Jewish people, past, present and future. The traditional rituals, blessings and customs provide continuity with the past. Innovative practices provide a personal dimension through which the uniqueness of the family can be expressed.

Different families will blend and balance the traditional and the innovative in different ways. What remains constant is the importance of recognizing that each new life is a symbol of the potential of all life. In accepting the blessings and the responsibilities of parenthood, we are given a unique opportunity to shape a life and nurture a soul, so that the children we are privileged to raise may increase the measure of holiness in our world, renew the work of creation and move the world closer to redemption.

For Further Reading

Jewish Lights Publishing has produced several books related to welcoming and raising children, including:

Celebrating Your New Jewish Daughter: Creating Jewish Ways to Welcome Baby Girls into the Covenant by Debra Nussbaum Cohen

The Jewish Pregnancy Book by Sandy Falk, MD, and Rabbi Daniel Judson, with Steven A. Rapp

The New Jewish Baby Album: Creating and Celebrating the Beginning of a Spiritual Life—A Jewish Lights Companion by the Editors at Jewish Lights

The New Jewish Baby Book: Names, Ceremonies & Customs—A Guide for Today's Families (2nd Edition) by Anita Diamant

Bible Baby Names: Spiritual Choices from Judeo-Christian Tradition by Anita Diamant

Lifecycles, volume 1: Jewish Women on Life Passages & Personal Milestones. Edited and with Introductions by Rabbi Debra Orenstein

Parenting as a Spiritual Journey: Deepening Ordinary & Extraordinary Events into Sacred Occasions by Rabbi Nancy Fuchs-Kreimer

Other Books of Interest

The Jewish Baby Handbook by Douglas Weber and Jessica Brodsky Weber (Behrman House)

Adoption and the Jewish Family: Contemporary Perspectives by Shelley Kapnek Rosenberg, (Jewish Publication Society)

Raising a Mensch: How to Bring Up Ethical Children in Today's World by Shelley Kapnek Rosenberg (Jewish Publication Society)

Reconstructionist Articles

(All articles from *The Reconstructionist* are available online at www.rrc.edu. Click "View Archive of *The Reconstructionist.*")

Shelley Kapnek Rosenberg, "Adoption and the Jewish Community: Like a Branch Transplanted," *The Reconstructionist,* Spring 2000

Michael Fessler: "Adoption and Jewish Families, A Proposal" *The Reconstructionist,* Fall 2001

Renee Bauer, "'Patrilineal Descent' and Same-Sex Parents: New Definitions of Identity," *The Reconstructionist,* Spring 2006

Jacob J. Staub, "'Bless us, Our Father'—Parenting and Our Images of God," *The Reconstructionist,* Spring 2000

Susan Schein, "From 'Two Civilizations' to Multiple Identities," *The Reconstructionist* Spring 2006

"Adoption & Conversion: A Reconstructionist Discussion," in *Reconstructionism Today,* Spring 2000 (available at www.jrf.org)

Prayers and Blessings

ON THE BIRTH OF A CHILD

בָּרוּךְ אַתָּה יהוה אֱלֹהֵינוּ רוּחַ הָעוֹלָם
שֶׁכָּכָה לוֹ בְּעוֹלָמוֹ:

Baruḥ atah adonay elo<u>heyn</u>u <u>ru</u>'ah ha'olam she<u>ka</u>ḥah lo be'olamo.

Blessed are you LIFE-GIVER our God, spirit of the world, in whose world such things exist.

Select from the following:

Parents: God of the generations, God of new beginnings, this child is your promise of tomorrow, made in your image, a reflection of your divine love. Teach us to be mother and father, worthy of this sacred trust of new life. Sustain us and our child in health and in love. We are thankful for the beauty of our lives together, which in a tender and powerful love has brought into the world a new life.

Parent: God of the generations, God of new beginnings, this is your promise of tomorrow, made in your image, a reflection of your divine love. Teach me to be a parent, worthy of this sacred trust of new life. Sustain me and my child in health and in love. I am thankful for the beauty of our lives together, which in a tender and powerful love has brought into the world a new life.

ON BIRTH OF A CHILD

Parents who have been assisted in conception may say:

בָּרוּךְ הָאִישׁ שֶׁהִתְחַלֵּק מִצַּלְמוֹ וְנָתַן לָנוּ/לִי
לְהַכִּיר אֶת הַחַיִּים:

Baruḥ ha'ish shehithḥalek mitzalmo venatan lanu/li lehakir et haḥayim.

Blessed is the man who has shared with us/me his divine spark and offered us/me the gift to nurture life.

בְּרוּכָה הָאִשָּׁה שֶׁמֵּרַחֲמָנוּת נָתְנָה לָנוּ/לִי
לְהַכִּיר אֶת הַחַיִּים:

Beruḥah ha'ishah shemeraḥmanut natenah lanu/li lehakir et haḥayim.

Blessed is the woman who from her womb-like compassion has shared with us/me the gift to nurture life.

On the birth of a child, one may recite:

נְבָרֵךְ אֶת עֵין הַחַיִּים עוֹשָׂה מַעֲשֵׂה בְרֵאשִׁית:

Nevareḥ et eyn haḥa'im osah ma'asey vereyshit.

Let us bless the Source of Life, who performs the mysteries of creation.

ON ADOPTION OF A CHILD

If two parents are present, continue here:
We have been blessed with the precious gift of a child. After so much waiting and hoping, we are filled with wonder and gratitude as we call you our child. You have grown to life apart from us, but now we hold you close to our hearts, lovingly cradle you in our arms, welcome you into the family circle and embrace you with the beauty of a rich tradition.

We dedicate ourselves to the creation of a Jewish home—a place of generosity, a place of compassion for others, a place of learning—in the hope that you will grow to cherish and carry on these ideals.

God of new beginnings, teach us to be parents worthy of this sacred trust of life. May our child grow in health, strong in mind and kind in heart, a lover of Torah, a seeker of peace. Bless all of us together within your shelter of shalom.

If one parent is present, continue here:
I have been blessed with the precious gift of a child. After so much waiting and hoping, I am filled with wonder and gratitude as I call you my child. You have grown to life apart from me, but now I hold you close to my heart, lovingly cradle you in my arms, welcome you into the family circle and embrace you with the beauty of a rich tradition.

I dedicate myself to the creation of a Jewish home—a place of generosity, a place of compassion for others, a place of learning—in the hope that you will grow to cherish and carry on these ideals.

God of new beginnings, teach me to be a parent worthy of this sacred trust of life. May my child grow in health, strong in mind and kind in heart, a lover of Torah, a seeker of peace. Bless all of us together within your shelter of shalom.

WHEN HOLDING A NEWBORN CHILD FOR THE FIRST TIME

God created the human in the divine image; in that image God created the human—male and female, God created them. God blessed them and said to them, "Be fruitful, and multiply, and fill up the earth!"

Blessed are you, The Incomparable our God, the sovereign of all worlds, who lets the mother rejoice in the fruit of her womb, and the father with his offspring.

וַיִּבְרָא אֱלֹהִים אֶת־הָאָדָם בְּצַלְמוֹ בְּצֶלֶם אֱלֹהִים בָּרָא אֹתוֹ זָכָר וּנְקֵבָה בָּרָא אֹתָם: וַיְבָרֶךְ אֹתָם אֱלֹהִים וַיֹּאמֶר לָהֶם פְּרוּ וּרְבוּ וּמִלְאוּ אֶת־הָאָרֶץ:

בָּרוּךְ אַתָּה יהוה אֱלֹהֵינוּ מֶלֶךְ הָעוֹלָם מְשַׂמֵּחַ הָאֵם בִּפְרִי בִטְנָהּ וּמֵגִיל הָאָב בְּיוֹצֵא חֲלָצָיו:

Vayivra elohim et ha'adam betzalmo betzelem elohim bara oto zaḥar unkevah bara otam. Vayvareḥ otam elohim vayomer lahem elohim peru urvu umilu et ha'aretz.

Baruḥ atah adonay eloheynu meleḥ ha'olam mesame'aḥ ha'em bifri vitnah umegil ha'av beyotzey ḥalatzav.

ON BRINGING A CHILD HOME FOR THE FIRST TIME

With joy and anticipation we bring our son/daughter into our home for the first time.

בָּרְכֵנוּ אָבִינוּ כֻּלָּנוּ כְּאֶחָד בְּאוֹר פָּנֶיךָ:

Bareḥenu avinu kulanu ke'eḥad be'or paneḥa.

Av Haraḥaman, may our life together be shaped by your Torah of life and deeds of lovingkindness.

As this child has been nurtured in the womb, so may we continue to feel your caring presence in our home. As we attend to his/her needs, grant us your protection and guidance.

May this home be a shelter for our child, a place where arms shall cradle him/her, and voices sing lullabies, where hands will uphold him/her and eyes delight in watching him/her grow.

In this home may we reach out to each other in love.
May our hearts be turned to each other.
May we create bonds of trust and care
that will keep us close
as we grow together as a family.

Bless us, NURTURING ONE,
all of us together in your light.
For in your light, EMBRACING ONE,
you have given us the Torah of life,
lovingkindness, justice, blessing,
caring, life and shalom.

ON WEANING A CHILD

Mother:

וַתִּתְפַּלֵּל חַנָּה וַתֹּאמַר
עָלַץ לִבִּי בַּיהוה
רָמָה קַרְנִי בַּיהוה
...כִּי שָׂמַחְתִּי בִּישׁוּעָתֶךָ:
אֵין־קָדוֹשׁ כַּיהוה
כִּי אֵין בִּלְתֶּךָ
וְאֵין צוּר כֵּאלֹהֵינוּ:

And Hannah prayed:

My heart exults in THE ETERNAL;
My strength is exalted in THE SOURCE.
...I rejoice in your salvation.

There is none holy like THE NURTURING ONE.
There is none besides you;
There is no rock like our God.

Parent/s:

בְּרוּכָה אַתְּ יָהּ עֵין הַחַיִּים
רוּחַ הָעוֹלָם שֶׁבָּרְאָה לְהַחֲיוֹת
נֶפֶשׁ כָּל חָי: בָּרוּךְ חֵי הָעוֹלָמִים הַזָּן אֶת
הָעוֹלָם בְּטוּבוֹ בְּחֵן בְּחֶסֶד וּבְרַחֲמִים:

Beruḥah at Yah, eyn haḥayim ru'aḥ ha'olam shebare'ah lehaḥayot nefesh kol ḥay. Baruḥ ḥey ha'olamim hazan et ha'olam betuvo beḥen beḥesed uvraḥamim.

Blessed are you YAH, the source of life, for all the means created to sustain life. Blessed is the Life of all the Worlds, who sustains the world with goodness, grace, lovingkindness and compassion.

Mother: Source of all life, I am grateful for the blessing of nursing which allows woman to share in the miracle of creation. My body has been attuned to the physical rhythm of new life forging spiritual bonds of love and trust.

Parent/s: Now the time of weaning has come, and we rejoice at this new sign of growth, this new chapter in your life. May we always be able to respond to your physical and spiritual needs and so help you to fulfill your potential for goodness. As you mature toward adulthood, may you follow the way of Torah and good deeds. May you grow strong in body, mind and spirit. May the strength, tenderness and joy that have filled these past months continue to sustain us as a family.

Biographies of Contributors

RABBI BENJAMIN BARNETT is the rabbi of Beit Am Jewish Community in Corvallis, Oregon.

RABBI KEVIN BERNSTEIN is a certified *mohel* and a consultant for the Mandel Center for Jewish Education at the JCC Association.

DANIEL GOLDMAN CEDARBAUM is a past-president of the Jewish Reconstructionist Federation, a member of the Jewish Reconstructionist Congregation in Evanston, Illinois, and an attorney in private practice.

RABBI RICHARD HIRSH is Executive Director of the Reconstructionist Rabbinical Association and teaches at the Reconstructionist Rabbinical College.

RABBI MYRIAM KLOTZ is Rabbinic Director of Yoga and Embodied Practices at the Institute of Jewish Spirituality, and Co-Director of the Yoga and Jewish Spirituality Teacher Training Certification Program. She is a spiritual director both at the Reconstructionist Rabbinical College and in private practice.

RABBI ILYSE S. KRAMER is a rabbi-educator involved in adult education teaching in a variety of denominational settings in the Greater Baltimore-Washington area. Her published curricular materials in Talmud and Jewish living are taught and studied in many communities.

RABBI NINA H. MANDEL is the rabbi of Congregation Beth El in Sunbury, Pennsylvania and a lecturer at Susquehanna University.

RABBI BARBARA ROSMAN PENZNER is the rabbi of Temple Hillel B'nai Torah in West Roxbury, Massachusetts and a past president of the Reconstructionist Rabbinical Association.

DR. SIMCHA RAPHAEL has been a death awareness educator for over twenty-five years. He works as a psychotherapist, affiliated with Mt. Airy Counseling Center, teaches in the Religion Departments of La Salle University and Temple University, and serves as a Spiritual Director at Reconstructionist Rabbinical College.

RABBI YAEL RIDBERG is the rabbi of West End Synagogue in New York City. She was the first Marshall T. Meyer Rabbinic Fellow at Congregation B'nai Jeshurun in New York.

RABBI SANDY EISENBERG SASSO is Senior Rabbi of Congregation Beth El Zedeck in Indianapolis, and an award-winning author of books for children.

RABBI JACOB J. STAUB is Professor of Jewish Philosophy and Spirituality at the Reconstructionist Rabbinical College. He is the co-author of *Exploring Judaism: A Reconstructionist Approach*.

RABBI DAVID A. TEUTSCH is the Wiener Professor of Contemporary Jewish Civilization and Director of the Levin-Lieber Program in Jewish Ethics at the Reconstructionist Rabbinical College. A past president of the College, he was Editor-in-Chief of the *Kol Haneshamah* prayerbook series.

ABIGAIL B. WEINBERG, a social and economic justice activist, is the Congregational Liaison for the Midwest Region of the Jewish Reconstructionist Federation, and a member of the Ann Arbor Reconstructionist Havurah in Ann Arbor, Michigan.

Index

Abraham 14, 25–26, 51, 59
Adoption 5, 10, 38, 49–50, 52–62, 63
Adoption (Judaism and) 52–62
Adoption (and conversion) 54–60
Adoption (and naming) 59–60
Adoption (identity and status) 49–50, 53–54, 57–58
Adoption (of infants) 5, 49
Adoptive parents 5, 50–56
Aliya 24, 30, 39-40
Ambilineal descent 6–9
Artificial insemination 17, 21
Ashkenazim 46
Assisted reproduction ix, 17
Avraham avinu 59–60

Bar/bat mitzva 19, 29, 41, 44, 57–58
Ben din 58
Biblical 16, 31, 41, 45, 48, 60
Bible 14, 24–25
B'diyavad 35
Birth (also see childbirth) 7, 10, 14, 16, 20–27, 29, 32, 38, 40–41, 44, 48–50, 52–57, 60, 62–63
Birth family 52, 54
Birth father 50, 53
Birth mother 17, 25, 50, 52–54, 57
Birth parents 14, 44, 53
Blessings 13, 16, 18–19, 21–22, 26, 30, 33, 39–40, 42–43, 50, 63, 67–70
Boy(s) 23, 25, 30–32, 36, 40–41, 43, 48, 54–55
Bris (see *brit mila*) 25, 36
Brit mila (also see *circumcision*) 15, 23–42, 44, 53–55, 61

Caesarean section 61–62
Childbirth 21–24, 38, 56
Christian, Christianity 15
Circumcision (also see *brit mila*) 15, 23, 25–38, 54–55
Community 4, 6–9, 11–12, 14, 16, 18–20, 24, 29, 32–34, 38, 40–41, 47, 50–51, 53–54, 56–57, 61, 63
Conception ix, 17–19, 21–24
Conservative Judaism 34
Conversion 8, 28, 50, 54–60
Conversion (of children) 8, 28, 50, 54–60
Covenant 14–15, 23, 25–27, 32, 35–36, 38–43, 54
Covenantal ceremonies 25–43
Custom(s) 3, 21–24, 26–31, 46, 58, 63

Daughter(s) 17, 23–24, 40–43, 46, 49–50, 61
Delivery 22, 29, 32
Descent 6–9, 46
Descent (patrilineal) 6–9
Descent (ambilineal) 6–9
Descent (matrilineal) 6–9

D'var shebikedusha 49

Egg donor 17
Elijah 26
Ethnic identity 9, 14–15, 45, 47

Family 4, 7, 11–12, 14, 16, 18, 20, 24, 26, 28–33, 43, 46, 48–56, 59, 62–63
Family (models of) 4, 20
Family (interfaith) 4, 51
Family (same-sex) 4, 8, 49
Family (single-parent) 4, 26, 50
Folk beliefs 22–23, 38
Foreskin 32
Foster parents 20

Gay and Lesbian 8
Gender 4, 26, 39–41, 47–48
Girl(s) 24, 39–43, 48, 54, 60
Godparent(s) 11, 30
Grandparents 8, 11, 26, 32, 50

Halakha (see Jewish law) 6, 9, 17, 36, 52–53, 58, 62
Hanuka 48
Hatafat dam brit 34–35, 54
Havdala 43
Hebrew names 44–51, 59
Holidays (*brit mila* on) 28
Holocaust 48
Hospital circumcision 25, 32–35, 55
Ḥupa 32, 43

Identity (also see Jewish identity) 6–9, 11, 14–15, 17, 20, 35, 38, 40, 44–45, 51–53, 56–59
Incest 17, 53
Israel 41, 53, 56, 60
Israelite people 14, 60

Interfaith (couples, families) 4, 51

Jewish calendar 27
Jewish identity x, 6–9, 15, 17, 20, 35, 38, 40, 44–45, 51–53, 56–59
Jewish status 6–9, 54, 58
Jewish law (also see *halakha*) 6, 26–27, 34–35, 52–53, 57

Klal Yisrael 57
Kohen, Kohanim 31, 53, 59–61
Kvatter 30
Kvatterin 30

Ladino 47
Legal issues 50, 52–58
Levi 53, 60–61
Lilith 22

Mamzer 53
Matrilineal descent 6–9
Matronymic 49–51, 59
Midrash 35–36, 41
Mikveh 28, 41–43, 49, 54–55, 58
Minhag, minhagim 46
Minyan 29
Miscarriage 22
Mishebeyrakh 24, 44
Mitzva 20, 28
Mohel, mohelet, mohalim 15, 26, 28–29, 31–32, 34–35, 37, 55

Names, naming 8, 14–15, 23–24, 26, 29, 32–33, 40–51, 53, 55, 59–61
Non-Jews 8, 17, 29–30, 50–51, 54, 57–59

Orthodox Judaism 24, 34, 53, 56

Patrilineal descent 6–9

Patronymic 49–51, 53, 59
Pesaḥ 26–28
Peter reḥem 61
Pidyon haben 61
Prayer 13, 21, 24, 26–27, 29, 33, 42, 44, 62, 67–70
Pregnancy 21–24
Procreation 16–20
P'ru Ur'vu 16–20

Rabbi 7, 9, 13, 16–17, 27–30, 33–35, 38, 41–43, 51, 54–58
Redemption (of first-born son) 60–62
Reform Judaism 8–9, 34, 55, 61
Reconstructionist Judaism ix–xi, 3–4, 8–9, 26, 33–34, 38, 50–51, 57–58, 60–62
Ritual 3, 9, 11–13, 15, 20–34, 36, 39–43, 49–50, 53, 56–58, 60–63
Rosh Hashana 28
Rosh Ḥodesh 41

Sandek 30–32
Same-sex partners 4, 8, 49
Sara imenu 59–60
Sefardim 46
Se'udat mitzva 30
Sexuality ix, 8, 18
Shabbat ix, 24, 26–28, 30, 33, 42–43, 60
Shavuot 28
Shulḥan Arukh 58
Son(s) 15, 17, 23, 25–26, 31, 36, 40–42, 47, 49–50, 53, 60–62
Sperm donor 17
Status 6–9
Sukkot 28
Synagogue 19, 24, 30, 39–42

Talmud 11, 16–17, 20
Torah 10, 12, 14–15, 35–36, 39, 43–44, 48, 60–61
Tzedaka 62

Weaning 21–24
Welcoming ceremony 10–13, 15, 29, 32, 39–43, 49, 61

Yiddish 16, 25, 45, 47
Yisrael 57, 60–61
Yom Kippur 28